meals in minutes

perfect pasta

RECIPES
Julia della Croce

PHOTOGRAPHS
Tucker + Hossler

weldon**owen**

contents

15 MINUTES HANDS-ON TIME

MAKE MORE TO STORE

about this book

Today's busy lifestyle leaves us little time in the kitchen, yet we still want to prepare delicious, healthy meals for our families and friends without a lot of fuss. Meals in Minutes *Perfect Pasta* is designed to help you do just that. This book will give you tips on planning, shopping for, and cooking great-tasting pasta dishes quickly and easily. The recipes are both inspired and deliberately uncomplicated, making cooking a pleasure and casual entertaining surprisingly easy.

Many of the recipes can be made in less than 30 minutes from start to finish, perfect for a weeknight supper. Some take less than 15 minutes of hands-on preparation, freeing up your time while the dish simmers on the stovetop. Others are made in big batches, which can be divided up and used for meals throughout the week. All three strategies illustrate smarter cooking, which is all about discovering ways to make life easier for the busy home cook without sacrificing quality.

30 minutes
start to finish

spaghetti alla carbonara

Olive oil, 3 tablespoons

Pancetta or bacon,
¼ lb (125 g), chopped

Garlic, 2 large cloves, minced

Dry white wine, ⅓ cup
(3 fl oz/80 ml)

Eggs, 3, at room temperature, beaten

Parmesan cheese, ⅓ cup
(1½ oz/45 g) freshly grated

Salt and freshly ground pepper

Spaghetti, 1 lb (500 g)

Fresh flat-leaf (Italian) parsley, ¼ cup (⅓ oz/10 g) minced

SERVES 4

1 **Make the sauce**
Bring a large pot of water to a boil. In a large frying pan over medium heat, warm 1 tablespoon of the oil. Add the pancetta and 3 tablespoons water and cook until the water has evaporated. Add the garlic and the remaining 2 tablespoons oil and cook, stirring occasionally, until the pancetta is browned, about 4 minutes. Stir in the wine and cook until most of the alcohol has evaporated, about 1 minute. In a large serving bowl, beat the eggs with the cheese and ¾ teaspoon salt; set aside.

2 **Cook the pasta**
Meanwhile, add 2 tablespoons salt and the pasta to the boiling water. Cook, stirring occasionally to prevent sticking, until al dente, according to the package directions. Drain, reserving about ½ cup (4 fl oz/125 ml) of the cooking water. Working quickly, add the pasta to the egg mixture and toss to coat. Add as much of the cooking water as needed to loosen the sauce. Add the pancetta, a generous amount of pepper, and the parsley. Toss again and serve.

cook's tip

The beauty of this classic dish
is its simplicity. You'll get the best
results if you use the highest-
quality ingredients, such as fresh
organic eggs, imported pancetta
or thick-sliced lean bacon,
and freshly grated Parmesan.

cook's tip

If broccoli rabe is not available,
use 1 ½ lb (750 g) broccoli
instead. Cut the broccoli into
small florets and reserve the
stalks for another use.

orecchiette with broccoli rabe

1 Make the sauce

Bring a large pot of water to a boil. Add 2 tablespoons salt and the broccoli rabe to the boiling water. Cover and cook until nearly tender, 4 minutes. Using a skimmer or slotted spoon, transfer to a bowl and set aside. Return the water to a boil. In a large frying pan over medium heat, warm the oil. Add the sausage and sauté, stirring occasionally, until browned, about 4 minutes. Drain off all but 4 tablespoons of fat from the pan. Add the garlic, ground fennel seed, and red pepper flakes and sauté until the garlic is fragrant, about 2 minutes. Add the broccoli rabe and stir to combine.

2 Cook the pasta

Meanwhile, add the pasta to the boiling water. Cook, stirring occasionally to prevent sticking, until al dente, according to the package directions. Drain, reserving about ½ cup (4 fl oz/ 125 ml) of the cooking water. Add the pasta to the sauce and stir to coat. Add as much of the reserved cooking water as needed to loosen the sauce, and serve.

Salt

Broccoli rabe, 1 bunch (1½ lb/750 g), trimmed and roughly chopped

Olive oil, ¼ cup (2 fl oz/60 ml)

Sweet Italian sausage, ¾ lb (375 g), casings removed and discarded, and meat crumbled

Garlic, 4 large cloves, minced

Ground fennel seed, ½ teaspoon

Red pepper flakes, pinch

Orecchiette, farfalle, or other medium-sized pasta, 1 lb (500 g)

SERVES 4

tagliatelle
with scallops

Lemons, 2

Bay or sea scallops, 1½ lb
(750 g), rinsed and patted dry

**Salt and freshly ground
pepper**

Unsalted butter,
8 tablespoons (4 oz/125 g),
at room temperature

Olive oil, 2 tablespoons

Garlic, 4 cloves, minced

Dry white wine, ⅔ cup
(5 fl oz/160 ml)

Tagliatelle or linguine,
1 lb (500 g)

Fresh chives, ¼ cup
(½ oz/15 g) finely snipped

Fresh bread crumbs,
3 tablespoons, lightly toasted

SERVES 4

1 Make the sauce

Bring a large pot of water to a boil. Grate 1 tablespoon zest and squeeze ⅓ cup (3 fl oz/80 ml) juice from the lemons; set aside. Season the scallops with salt and pepper. In a large frying pan over medium heat, melt 4 tablespoons of the butter with the olive oil. Add the garlic and sauté until fragrant, about 2 minutes. Add the scallops and cook, turning once, until golden, about 2 minutes per side. Add the lemon juice and wine and cook until most of the alcohol has evaporated, about 1 minute. Add ½ teaspoon each salt and pepper, and toss. Add the remaining 4 tablespoons butter and the lemon zest. Toss to combine and set aside.

2 Cook the pasta

Meanwhile, add 2 tablespoons salt and the pasta to the boiling water. Cook, stirring occasionally to prevent sticking, until al dente, according to the package directions. Drain, reserving about ½ cup (4 fl oz/125 ml) of the cooking water. Add the pasta to the sauce. Add as much of the cooking water as needed to loosen the sauce, along with the chives and bread crumbs. Toss to combine and serve.

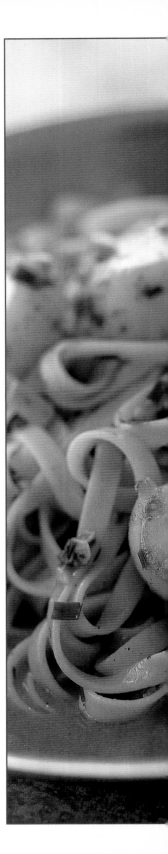

cook's tip

Whenever you have leftover day-old bread, preferably a baguette or rustic white loaf, cut it into slices, place on a baking sheet, and dry out the slices in the oven at 300°F (150°C) for about 10 minutes. Process the toasted bread in a food processor to make crumbs. Store the crumbs in an airtight container in the freezer for up to 4 months.

cook's tip

Grating garlic using a rasp-style grater is faster and easier than mincing it with a knife. Make sure to use a grater with medium to large holes. Be vigilant when sautéing grated garlic as it can burn easily.

rigatoni with mushroom ragù

1 Make the sauce

Bring a large pot of water to a boil. Soak the dried porcini in 1 cup (8 fl oz/250 ml) hot water for 10 minutes. Strain through a fine-mesh sieve, and set both the liquid and mushrooms aside. In a large frying pan over medium heat, melt the butter with the oil. Add the garlic and rosemary and sauté until fragrant, about 1 minute. Add the onion and sauté until softened, about 3 minutes. Add the reserved porcini and fresh mushrooms and cook, stirring frequently, until they release some of their liquid, about 5 minutes. Add the wine, reduce the heat to medium-low, and cook until most of the alcohol has evaporated, about 1 minute. Add the tomato paste, reserved mushroom liquid, and broth, and continue to cook, stirring occasionally, until the flavors have blended, about 10 minutes. Remove and discard the rosemary sprig and season to taste with salt and pepper.

2 Cook the pasta

Meanwhile, add 2 tablespoons salt and the pasta to the boiling water. Cook, stirring occasionally to prevent sticking, until al dente, according to the package directions. Drain and add to the sauce. Warm briefly over low heat to blend the flavors and serve.

Dried porcini mushrooms (ceps), ½ oz (15 g)

Unsalted butter, 2 tablespoons

Olive oil, 3 tablespoons

Garlic, 4 large cloves, minced

Fresh rosemary, 1 sprig, 4 inches (10 cm) long

Yellow onion, 1 small, finely chopped

Mixed fresh mushrooms, such as shiitake, oyster, chanterelle, and cremini, ½ lb (250 g), thinly sliced

Dry red wine, ½ cup (4 fl oz/125 ml)

Tomato paste, 3 tablespoons

Chicken or beef broth, 1 cup (8 fl oz/250 ml)

Salt and freshly ground pepper

Rigatoni, 1 lb (500 g)

SERVES 4

spaghettini with olive pesto

Olive oil, ½ cup (4 fl oz/ 125 ml), plus more for drizzling

Garlic, 1 small clove, minced

Black olives, ½ lb (250 g), pitted and coarsely chopped

Green olives, ½ lb (250 g), pitted and coarsely chopped

Fresh marjoram, 1 teaspoon minced, or ½ teaspoon dried

Salt and freshly ground pepper

Spaghettini or spaghetti, 1 lb (500 g)

Fresh flat-leaf (Italian) parsley, ¼ cup (⅓ oz/10 g) minced

SERVES 4

1 Make the pesto

Bring a large pot of water to a boil. In a food processor, combine the ½ cup oil, garlic, olives, and marjoram. Pulse to combine. Using a rubber spatula, scrape down the sides of the bowl, and then pulse once or twice more to form a coarse sauce. Transfer the olive pesto to a large bowl.

2 Cook the pasta

Meanwhile, add 2 tablespoons salt and the pasta to the boiling water. Cook, stirring occasionally to prevent sticking, until al dente, according to the package directions. Drain, reserving about ½ cup (4 fl oz/125 ml) of the cooking water. Add the pasta to the pesto along with the parsley. Toss to combine. Add as much of the reserved cooking water as needed to loosen the sauce. Season to taste with salt and pepper and serve.

cook's tip

You can pit olives quickly using the back of a large knife. Put the olives on a cutting board and lay the widest part of the blade on top, sharp edge facing away from you. Carefully roll the olives, pressing down on the blade. The olives should split, allowing you to remove the pits easily.

cook's tip

For a classic baked macaroni and
cheese, preheat the oven to 400°F
(200°C). Increase the milk by
¼ cup (2 fl oz/60 ml). Undercook
the pasta by 2 minutes, drain,
and add to the sauce. Pour into
a buttered baking dish. Sprinkle
with ½ cup (1 oz/30 g) bread
crumbs, and bake until golden
brown, 10–12 minutes.

three-cheese
macaroni

1 Make the sauce

Bring a large pot of water to a boil. In a small saucepan over medium heat, warm the milk until small bubbles begin to form around the edge of the pan. Remove from the heat. In a large saucepan over low heat, melt the butter. Add the flour a little at a time, whisking to incorporate. Raise the heat to medium-low and very gradually whisk in the hot milk. Cook, stirring frequently, until the mixture is thick and creamy, about 15 minutes. Add the Gruyère, the Fontina, salt to taste, and the cayenne, if using. Cook, stirring frequently, until the cheeses are melted, about 2 minutes. Stir in the Parmesan, and set the sauce aside.

2 Cook the pasta

Meanwhile, add 2 tablespoons salt and the pasta to the boiling water. Cook, stirring occasionally to prevent sticking, until al dente, according to the package directions. Drain and add to the sauce. Stir to combine and serve.

Milk, 3 cups (24 fl oz/750 ml)

Unsalted butter,
5 tablespoons (2½ oz/75 g)

Flour, 3 tablespoons

Gruyère cheese, ¾ cup
(3 oz/90 g) shredded

Fontina cheese, ¾ cup
(3 oz/90 g) shredded

Salt

Cayenne pepper,
¼ teaspoon (optional)

Parmesan cheese, ½ cup
(2 oz/60 g) freshly grated

Macaroni, shells, or penne,
1 lb (500 g)

SERVES 4

tagliatelle with crab & tarragon

Unsalted butter,
4 tablespoons (2 oz/60 g)

Olive oil, 2 tablespoons

Leek, 1, white and pale green parts, halved, rinsed, and thinly sliced

Shallot, 1 large, minced

Lump crabmeat, ¾ lb (375 g), picked over for shell fragments

Dry white wine, ½ cup (4 fl oz/125 ml)

Fresh tarragon, 3 tablespoons minced

Heavy (double) cream, 1 cup (8 fl oz/250 ml)

Salt and white pepper

Tagliatelle or linguine, 1 lb (500 g)

SERVES 4

1 Make the sauce
Bring a large pot of water to a boil. In a large frying pan over medium heat, melt the butter with the oil. Add the leek and shallot and sauté until softened, about 7 minutes. Add the crabmeat and cook, stirring occasionally, until just warmed through, about 4 minutes. Add the wine and cook until most of the alcohol has evaporated, about 1 minute. Reduce the heat to medium-low and add half of the tarragon, the cream, and 1 teaspoon salt. Cook until the sauce is warmed through, about 3 minutes. Do not let it boil. Remove from the heat.

2 Cook the pasta
Meanwhile, add 2 tablespoons salt and the pasta to the boiling water. Cook, stirring occasionally to prevent sticking, until al dente, according to the package directions. Drain, reserving about ½ cup (4 fl oz/125 ml) of the cooking water. Add the pasta to the sauce and toss to combine. Add as much of the reserved cooking water as needed to loosen the sauce. Sprinkle with the remaining tarragon, season to taste with pepper, and serve.

cook's tip

To quickly cut a zucchini into matchsticks, trim the ends, slice the zucchini lengthwise into ¼-inch (6-mm) slices, then cut it crosswise into thirds. Cut each stack lengthwise into thin strips.

fusilli with zucchini & goat cheese

1 **Make the sauce**
Bring a large pot of water to a boil. In a large frying pan over medium-low heat, warm the oil. Add the garlic and sauté until fragrant, about 2 minutes. Raise the heat to medium-high, add the zucchini, and sauté until lightly browned, about 10 minutes. Remove from the heat, add 1 teaspoon salt and the goat cheese, and toss to combine.

2 **Cook the pasta**
Meanwhile, add 2 tablespoons salt and the pasta to the boiling water. Cook, stirring occasionally to prevent sticking, until al dente, according to the package directions. Drain, reserving about ½ cup (4 fl oz/125 ml) of the cooking water. Add the pasta to the sauce along with the herbs and a generous amount of pepper. Toss to combine. Add as much of the cooking water as needed to loosen the sauce and serve.

Olive oil, ½ cup (4 fl oz/125 ml)

Garlic, 4 large cloves, thinly sliced

Zucchini (courgettes), 3 small, trimmed and cut into matchsticks

Salt and freshly ground pepper

Goat cheese, ¼ lb (125 g)

Fusilli or other spiral pasta, 1 lb (500 g)

Fresh flat-leaf (Italian) parsley, ¼ cup (⅓ oz/10 g) minced

Fresh basil, ⅓ cup (½ oz/15 g) slivered

SERVES 4

25

penne with vodka sauce

Unsalted butter,
4 tablespoons (2 oz/60 g)

Heavy (double) cream,
1 cup (8 fl oz/250 ml)

Tomato paste, ¼ cup
(2 oz/60 g)

Vodka, ⅓ cup (3 fl oz/80 ml)
plus 2 tablespoons

Fresh basil, 2 tablespoons
slivered

Red pepper flakes, pinch

Salt

**Penne or other tubular
pasta,** 1 lb (500 g)

Parmesan cheese, ½ cup
(2 oz/60 g) freshly grated

SERVES 4

1 Make the sauce
Bring a large pot of water to a boil. In a large frying pan over medium-low heat, melt the butter with the cream. In a small bowl, dissolve the tomato paste in the vodka. Stir into the cream mixture. Add the basil and red pepper flakes. Season with 1 teaspoon salt. Cook until most of the alcohol has evaporated and the sauce is thick enough to coat the back of a spoon, about 5 minutes.

2 Cook the pasta
Meanwhile, add 2 tablespoons salt and the pasta to the boiling water. Cook, stirring occasionally to prevent sticking, until al dente, according to the package directions. Drain, reserving about ½ cup (4 fl oz/125 ml) of the cooking water. Add the pasta to the sauce and warm briefly over low heat to blend the flavors. Add the Parmesan and toss to combine. Add as much of the cooking water as needed to loosen the sauce and serve.

cook's tip

For a new spin on classic
vodka sauce, add a splash of
brandy or Cognac to the ⅓ cup
vodka in place of the extra
2 tablespoons vodka.

cook's tip

If you are unable to find escarole, you can substitute another bitter green such as mustard greens or chicory (curly endive). Core and roughly chop either vegetable before cooking.

pasta with beans & escarole

1 Make the sauce

Bring a large pot of water to a boil. In a large frying pan over low heat, warm the oil. Add the garlic and sauté until fragrant, about 2 minutes. Raise the heat to medium-low, add the pancetta, and sauté until lightly browned, about 5 minutes. Raise the heat to medium, add the escarole, and cook until wilted, about 2 minutes. Add the broth, beans, marjoram, and red pepper flakes. Season to taste with salt. Reduce the heat to low, cover, and cook until the beans are heated through, about 5 minutes.

2 Cook the pasta

Meanwhile, add 2 tablespoons salt and the pasta to the boiling water. Cook, stirring occasionally to prevent sticking, until al dente, according to the package directions. Drain, reserving about ½ cup (4 fl oz/125 ml) of the cooking water. Add the pasta to the sauce and toss to combine. Warm briefly over low heat to blend the flavors. Add as much of the cooking water as needed to loosen the sauce and serve.

Olive oil, ½ cup (4 fl oz/125 ml)

Garlic, 4 large cloves, minced

Pancetta or bacon, 2 oz (60 g), chopped

Escarole, 1 head, cored and trimmed, leaves cut into strips

Chicken broth, ¾ cup (6 fl oz/180 ml)

White beans, 1 can (14 oz/ 440 g), drained and rinsed

Fresh marjoram, 1 tablespoon minced

Red pepper flakes, pinch

Salt

Small tubular pasta, such as ditali, ¾ lb (375 g)

SERVES 4

cappellini with lemon, garlic & parsley

Olive oil, ½ cup
(4 fl oz/125 ml)

Garlic, 4 large cloves, minced

Lemon zest, from 1 lemon

Lemon juice, from ½ lemon

Salt and freshly ground pepper

Cappellini or spaghettini,
1 lb (500 g)

Fresh flat-leaf (Italian) parsley, ½ cup (¾ oz/20 g) minced

SERVES 4

1 Make the sauce
Bring a large pot of water to a boil. In a large frying pan over low heat, warm the oil. Add the garlic and sauté until fragrant but not golden, 1–2 minutes. Remove from the heat and stir in the lemon zest, lemon juice, and 1 teaspoon salt. Season to taste with pepper. Transfer to a large serving bowl.

2 Cook the pasta
Meanwhile, add 2 tablespoons salt and the pasta to the boiling water. Cook, stirring occasionally to prevent sticking, until al dente, according to the package directions. Drain, reserving about ½ cup (4 fl oz/125 ml) of the cooking water. Add the pasta to the sauce along with the minced parsley and toss to combine. Add as much of the cooking water as needed to loosen the sauce. Season to taste with salt and pepper and serve.

cook's tip

For colorful and flavorful variations, add ½ cup (3 oz/ 90 g) halved cherry tomatoes; ½ cup (2½ oz/75 g) chopped, pitted black or green olives; or 1 tablespoon each minced fresh thyme, rosemary, and sage to the pasta when you add the parsley.

cook's tip

The cauliflower can be cooked in
advance and stored in an airtight
container in the refrigerator for
up to 2 days. It's a good idea
to save the cooking water, too,
as it will add flavor to the dish.
Boil the pasta in the reserved
cauliflower water when you are
ready to complete this recipe.

pasta shells with cauliflower

1 Cook the cauliflower

Bring a large pot of water to a boil. Add 2 tablespoons salt and the cauliflower to the boiling water and cook until tender, about 7 minutes. Using a skimmer or slotted spoon, transfer the cauliflower to a colander to drain; set aside. Return the water to a boil.

2 Make the sauce

In a large frying pan over medium-low heat, warm 4 tablespoons of the oil. Add the garlic, green onions, marjoram, and red pepper flakes and sauté until the onions are wilted, about 4 minutes. Stir in the cauliflower, parsley, and broth. Raise the heat to medium and cook, stirring constantly, until the cauliflower is lightly colored and the liquid is slightly reduced, about 12 minutes.

3 Cook the pasta

Meanwhile, add the pasta to the boiling water and cook, stirring occasionally to prevent sticking, until al dente, according to the package directions. Drain, reserving about ½ cup (4 fl oz/125 ml) of the cooking water. Add the pasta to the sauce, and toss to combine. Add as much of the cooking water as needed to loosen the sauce. In a small frying pan over medium heat, warm the remaining 4 tablespoons oil. Add the bread crumbs and cook, stirring frequently, until golden, about 2 minutes. Sprinkle the bread crumbs over the pasta and serve.

Salt

Cauliflower, 1 medium head, cut into florets, then coarsely chopped

Olive oil, 8 tablespoons (4 fl oz/125 ml)

Garlic, 4 large cloves, minced

Green (spring) onions, 6–8, white and tender green parts, thinly sliced

Fresh marjoram, 2 teaspoons minced

Red pepper flakes, ½ teaspoon

Fresh flat-leaf (Italian) parsley, 3 tablespoons minced

Chicken or vegetable broth, 2 cups (16 fl oz/ 500 ml)

Conchiglie or other small pasta shells, ¾ lb (375 g)

Fresh bread crumbs, ¼ cup (½ oz/15 g)

SERVES 4

33

linguine
with clams

Olive oil, ½ cup
(4 fl oz/125 ml)

Garlic, 5 large cloves, minced

Red pepper flakes,
¼ teaspoon

**Small clams such as
littleneck or Manila,**
3½ lb (1.75 kg), scrubbed

Dry white wine, ½ cup
(4 fl oz/125 ml)

Salt

**Fresh flat-leaf (Italian)
parsley,** ⅓ cup (½ oz/15 g)
finely chopped

Linguine or spaghetti,
1 lb (500 g)

SERVES 4

1 **Cook the clams**
Bring a large pot of of water to a boil. In a large frying pan over medium-low heat, warm the oil, garlic, and red pepper flakes until the garlic is fragrant, about 3 minutes. Discard any clams that fail to close to the touch. Add the clams, the wine, and 1 teaspoon salt and cover with a tight-fitting lid. Raise the heat to medium and cook, shaking the pan vigorously and often, until the clams open, about 10 minutes. Use a wooden spoon to stir the clams, discarding any empty shells and any unopened clams. Add the parsley. Remove from the heat.

2 **Cook the pasta**
Meanwhile, add 2 tablespoons salt and the pasta to the boiling water. Cook, stirring occasionally to prevent sticking, until al dente, according to the package directions. Drain, add the pasta to the clams, and toss to combine. Warm briefly over low heat to blend the flavors and serve.

cook's tip

Medium-sized shrimp (prawns) can be substituted for the clams. Peel and devein 1 1/2 lb (750 g) shrimp, leaving the tails intact. Cook the shrimp with the garlic until they turn opaque, about 3 minutes, then finish the recipe as directed.

cook's tip

For a more earthy, robust flavor,
use a mixture of cultivated
and wild mushrooms, such as
shiitake, enoki, porcini, and
chanterelle.

pappardelle
with mushrooms

1 **Make the sauce**
Bring a large pot of water to a boil. In a large frying pan over medium heat, warm the oil. Add the pancetta and sauté until lightly browned, about 3 minutes. Add the shallots and sauté until lightly golden, about 3 minutes. Add the mushrooms and cook until they have softened and released most of their liquid, about 5 minutes. Add the goat cheese and stir to combine. Stir in the wine and cook until most of the alcohol has evaporated, about 1 minute. Season to taste with salt and pepper.

2 **Cook the pasta**
Meanwhile, add 2 tablespoons salt and the pasta to the boiling water. Cook, stirring occasionally to prevent sticking, until al dente, according to the package directions. Drain, reserving about ½ cup (4 fl oz/125 ml) of the cooking water. Add the pasta to the sauce along with the tarragon. Toss to combine. Warm briefly over low heat to blend the flavors. Add as much of the cooking water as needed to loosen the sauce and serve.

Olive oil, ¼ cup (2 fl oz/60 ml)

Pancetta or bacon, 3 oz (90 g), chopped

Shallots, 3 large, minced

Cremini or button mushrooms, 10 oz (315 g), thinly sliced

Goat cheese, ¼ lb (125 g)

Dry white wine, ½ cup (4 fl oz/125 ml)

Salt and freshly ground pepper

Pappardelle or wide egg noodles, 1 lb (500 g)

Fresh tarragon, ¼ cup (⅓ oz/10 g) minced

SERVES 4

spaghetti with mixed seafood

Olive oil, ⅓ cup (3 fl oz/80 ml)

Garlic, 3 large cloves, thinly sliced

Shallot, 1 large, minced

Red pepper flakes, ¼ teaspoon

Large shrimp (prawns), ½ lb (250 g), peeled and deveined, tails intact

Dry white wine, ½ cup (4 fl oz/125 ml)

Small clams such as littleneck or Manila, ½ lb (250 g), scrubbed

Mussels, ½ lb (250 g), scrubbed and debearded if necessary

Lump crabmeat, ½ lb (250 g), picked over for shell fragments

Salt

Spaghetti or linguine, 1 lb (500 g)

Fresh basil, ⅓ cup (½ oz/15 g) minced

SERVES 4

1 Cook the seafood

Bring a large pot of water to a boil. In a large frying pan over medium-low heat, warm the oil. Add the garlic, shallot, and red pepper flakes and sauté until fragrant and softened, about 2 minutes. Add the shrimp and sauté until they are just opaque throughout, about 3 minutes. Using a slotted spoon, remove the shrimp from the pan and set aside. Add the wine, clams, and mussels to the pan, discarding any mussels or clams that fail to close to the touch. Raise the heat to medium, cover, and cook, shaking the pan occasionally, until the clams and mussels open, about 10 minutes. Discard any empty shells and any unopened clams or mussels. Add the shrimp back to the pan along with the crabmeat and warm briefly to blend the flavors, about 3 minutes.

2 Cook the pasta

Meanwhile, add 2 tablespoons salt and the pasta to the boiling water. Cook, stirring occasionally to prevent sticking. When the pasta is not quite al dente, about 1 minute less than the package directions, drain, reserving about ½ cup (4 fl oz/ 125 ml) of the cooking water. Add the pasta to the sauce along with the basil. Toss to combine. Warm briefly over low heat to blend the flavors. Add as much of the cooking water as needed to loosen the sauce and serve.

cook's tip

When cooking with shrimp and crab, save the shells to use later in fish stock. Store the shells in an airtight container in the freezer for up to 1 month.

cook's tip

Instead of the Swiss chard, you
can use 2 cups (4 oz/125 g)
chopped baby or regular spinach
leaves. Reduce the cooking time
from 7 minutes to 4 minutes.

whole wheat fettuccine with chard

1 Make the sauce
Bring a large pot of water to a boil. In a large frying pan over medium heat, warm the oil. Add the pancetta and sauté until browned, about 10 minutes. Transfer to paper towels to drain. Add the garlic and sauté until fragrant, about 1 minute. Add the chard and broth, cover, reduce the heat to medium-low, and cook, stirring occasionally, until the chard is wilted and the flavors have melded, about 7 minutes.

2 Cook the pasta
Meanwhile, add 2 tablespoons salt and the pasta to the boiling water. Cook, stirring occasionally to prevent sticking, until al dente, according to the package directions. Drain and add it to the chard. Add the reserved pancetta, the butter, and the Gorgonzola and toss to combine. Warm briefly over low heat to melt the Gorgonzola and blend the flavors. Season to taste with salt and pepper and serve.

Olive oil, 1 tablespoon

Pancetta or bacon, 6 oz (185 g), chopped

Garlic, 2 cloves, minced

Swiss chard, ¾ lb (375 g), ribs removed, leaves cut crosswise into thin strips

Chicken broth, ¾ cup (6 fl oz/180 ml)

Salt and freshly ground pepper

Whole wheat (wholemeal) fettuccine or linguine, ¾ lb (375 g)

Unsalted butter, 4 tablespoons (2 oz/60 g), cut into chunks, at room temperature

Mild Gorgonzola cheese, ¼ lb (125 g), crumbled

SERVES 4

41

gemelli with brown butter & asparagus

Salt and freshly ground pepper

Asparagus, 1 lb (500 g), trimmed and cut into 1-inch (2.5-cm) pieces

Unsalted butter, ½ cup (4 oz/125 g)

Hazelnuts (filberts), 1 cup (5 oz/155 g), toasted, skinned, and coarsely chopped

Gemelli or other short pasta such as penne, 1 lb (500 g)

Parmesan cheese, ½ cup (4 oz/125 g) freshly grated

SERVES 4

1 **Blanch the asparagus**
Bring a large pot of water to a boil. Add 2 tablespoons salt and the asparagus to the boiling water and cook just until tender, about 4 minutes. Using a skimmer or slotted spoon, transfer the asparagus to a colander and drain; set aside. Return the water to a boil.

2 **Make the sauce**
In a large frying pan over low heat, melt the butter. When it stops foaming and the solids begin to separate, use a shallow spoon to skim off most of the solids. Cook until the butter is lightly browned, about 2 minutes; be careful that it doesn't burn. Add the hazelnuts and season to taste with salt. Add the asparagus and toss. Remove from the heat.

3 **Cook the pasta**
Meanwhile, add the pasta to the boiling water. Cook, stirring occasionally to prevent sticking, until al dente, according to the package directions. Drain, reserving about ½ cup (4 fl oz/ 125 ml) of the cooking water. Add the pasta to the sauce and toss to combine. Warm briefly over low heat to blend the flavors. Add as much of the cooking water as needed to loosen the sauce. Season to taste with salt and pepper. Top with the Parmesan and serve.

cook's tip

The success of this simple,
creamy sauce depends upon the
cheese. Use a young, very mild
Gorgonzola, often called *dolce*.
Aged Gorgonzola is too strong
for this sauce.

creamy penne with walnuts

1 Make the sauce

Bring a large pot of water to a boil. In a large frying pan over medium-low heat, melt the butter. Stir in the Gorgonzola, mashing it with a wooden spoon. Add the cream. Bring to a gentle simmer, stirring occasionally. Reduce the heat to low and cook, stirring, until the sauce is thick enough to coat the back of a spoon, about 3 minutes. Do not allow the sauce to boil. Remove from the heat and stir in the Parmesan and ½ teaspoon pepper.

2 Cook the pasta

Meanwhile, add 2 tablespoons salt and the pasta to the boiling water. Cook, stirring occasionally to prevent sticking, until al dente, according to the package directions. Drain, reserving about ½ cup (4 fl oz/125 ml) of the cooking water. Add the pasta to the sauce along with the walnuts and stir to combine. Add as much of the cooking water as needed to loosen the sauce. Warm briefly over low heat to blend the flavors and serve.

Unsalted butter,
4 tablespoons (2 oz/60 g)

Mild Gorgonzola cheese,
6 oz (185 g)

Heavy (double) cream,
1 cup (8 fl oz/250 ml)

Parmesan cheese, ¾ cup
(3 oz/90 g) freshly grated

Salt and freshly ground pepper

Penne or other tubular pasta, 1 lb (500 g)

Walnuts, ½ cup (2 oz/
60 g), lightly toasted and
coarsely chopped

SERVES 4

pappardelle
in herb broth

Unsalted butter,
2 tablespoons

Pancetta or bacon, 3 oz
(90 g), chopped

Shallots, 3, minced

Green (spring) onions,
6–8, white and tender green
parts, thinly sliced

Chicken broth, 7 cups
(56 fl oz/1.75 l)

**Fresh or frozen petite
peas,** 10 oz (315 g)

**Pappardelle or wide egg
noodles,** ¾ lb (375 g)

**Fresh flat-leaf (Italian)
parsley,** 3 tablespoons
minced

Fresh mint, 2 tablespoons
minced

Fresh chives, 2 tablespoons
finely snipped

**Salt and freshly ground
pepper**

Parmesan cheese, 1 cup
(4 oz/125 g) freshly grated

SERVES 4

1 Make the soup base
In a large pot over medium-low heat, melt the butter. Add the pancetta and sauté until slightly browned, about 5 minutes. Add the shallots and green onions and sauté until softened, about 3 minutes. Raise the heat to medium, add the broth, and bring to a simmer. Cover and cook until the flavors have blended, about 5 minutes.

2 Finish the dish
Add the peas and pasta to the soup and cook until the pasta is not quite al dente, about 2 minutes less than the package directions. The pasta will continue to cook in the heat of the soup. Stir in the parsley, mint, and chives. Warm briefly over low heat to blend the flavors. Season to taste with salt and pepper. Ladle the soup into bowls and serve, passing the Parmesan at the table.

cook's tip

If you prefer, substitute 3 oz (90 g) cubed cooked ham for the pancetta. The firm texture of the ham works well in this soup.

cook's tip

To toast pine nuts quickly, heat
a cast-iron or heavy-bottomed
frying pan over medium-high
heat until hot. Add the pine nuts,
turn off the heat, and cook,
stirring occasionally, until golden
and fragrant, about 10 minutes.

farfalle with veal & pine nuts

1 Brown the veal

Bring a large pot of water to a boil. Place the flour, 1 teaspoon salt, and ½ teaspoon pepper in a resealable plastic bag. Add the veal and shake to coat the meat evenly. In a large frying pan over medium-high heat, melt the butter with the oil. Remove the veal from the bag, shaking off the excess flour. Add the veal, in batches if necessary to avoid crowding, and sauté until browned, about 6 minutes total. Remove the veal from the pan and set aside.

2 Make the sauce

Place the same pan over medium-low heat. Add the wine, lemon zest, and rosemary and stir, scraping up the brown bits from the bottom of the pan. Cook until most of the alcohol has evaporated, about 1 minute. Add the broth and bring to a simmer. Reduce the heat to medium-low and cook until the flavors are blended, about 10 minutes. Return the veal and any accumulated juices to the pan, add the pine nuts, and cook until warmed through. Season to taste with salt and pepper.

3 Cook the pasta

Meanwhile, add 2 tablespoons salt and the pasta to the boiling water. Cook, stirring occasionally to prevent sticking, until al dente, according to the package directions. Drain, reserving ½ cup (4 fl oz/125 ml) of the cooking water. Add the pasta to the sauce and toss to combine. Warm briefly over low heat to blend the flavors. Add as much of the reserved cooking water as needed to loosen the sauce and serve.

Flour, ¼ cup (1½ oz/45 g)

Salt and freshly ground pepper

Veal scallopine, 1 lb (500 g), cut into small pieces

Unsalted butter, ½ cup (4 oz/125 g)

Olive oil, 2 tablespoons

Dry white wine, ¾ cup (6 fl oz/180 ml)

Lemon zest, from 1 lemon

Fresh rosemary, 1 teaspoon minced

Chicken broth, 1½ cups (12 fl oz/375 ml)

Pine nuts, 3 tablespoons, toasted

Farfalle or other medium-sized pasta, 1 lb (500 g)

SERVES 4

49

15 minutes
hands-on time

spaghetti all'amatriciana

Olive oil, 2 tablespoons

Yellow onion, 1 small, finely chopped

Pancetta or bacon, 3 oz (90 g), chopped

Red pepper flakes, ¼ teaspoon

Dry white wine, ½ cup (4 fl oz/125 ml)

Tomato paste, 2 tablespoons

Canned whole plum (Roma) tomatoes, 2½ cups (20 fl oz/625 ml), chopped, with juice

Salt

Spaghetti, 1 lb (500 g)

Aged pecorino romano or Parmesan cheese, ½ cup (2 oz/60 g) freshly grated

SERVES 4

1 **Make the sauce**
Bring a large pot of water to a boil. In a large frying pan over medium-low heat, warm the oil. Add the onion, pancetta, and red pepper flakes and sauté until the onion is softened and the pancetta is lightly browned, about 6 minutes. Stir in the wine and the tomato paste. Reduce the heat to low and cook until most of the alcohol has evaporated, about 1 minute. Add the tomatoes and ½ teaspoon salt. Raise the heat to medium-low and simmer, uncovered, stirring occasionally, until the sauce is thickened, about 20 minutes.

2 **Cook the pasta**
Meanwhile, add 2 tablespoons salt and the pasta to the boiling water. Cook, stirring occasionally to prevent sticking, until al dente, according to the package directions. Drain, reserving about ½ cup (4 fl oz/125 ml) of cooking water. Add the pasta to the sauce and toss well to coat. Sprinkle with a third of the pecorino romano and toss again. Add as much of the cooking water as needed to loosen the sauce. Serve, passing the remaining cheese at the table.

cook's tip

Simple sauces such as this one
and Spaghetti alla Puttanesca
(page 64) can easily be doubled
or even tripled. Serve one batch
of the sauce tonight with spaghetti
or another pasta and save the
rest to ladle over purchased fresh
ravioli or tortelloni another night.

cook's tip

In a simple, rustic dish such
as this one, it is important to use
the best ingredients. Look for
premium extra-virgin olive oil
with a greenish tint and peppery
kick for drizzling on top.

pasta with chickpeas

1 Simmer the chickpeas

In a large pot over medium-high heat, combine the chickpeas and the broth. Bring to a boil, reduce the heat to low, and cook, partially covered, until the chickpeas are very tender, about 15 minutes. Remove 1 cup (7 oz/220 g) of the chickpeas and pass them through a potato ricer or purée in a food processor or blender. Return to the pot and stir.

2 Make the soup

In a frying pan over medium-low heat, warm the 3 tablespoons oil. Add the pancetta and sauté until lightly browned, about 3 minutes. Stir in the onion, garlic, and sage, and sauté until the vegetables are softened, about 2 minutes. Add the tomato paste and ½ cup (4 fl oz/125 ml) of the chickpea broth and stir to combine. Add the pancetta mixture to the pot with the chickpeas. Bring to a gentle boil over medium heat and cook for about 10 minutes. Add the pasta and cook, stirring frequently, until al dente, about 4 minutes. Season to taste with salt and pepper. Ladle the soup into bowls, drizzle with olive oil, sprinkle with the parsley, and serve.

Canned chickpeas (garbanzo beans), 4 cups (28 oz/875 g), drained and rinsed

Chicken broth, 8 cups (64 fl oz/2 l)

Olive oil, 3 tablespoons, plus more for drizzling

Pancetta or bacon, 3 oz (90 g), chopped

Yellow onion, 1, chopped

Garlic, 3 large cloves, minced

Fresh sage or rosemary, 1 tablespoon minced

Tomato paste, 2 tablespoons

Ditali or other small soup pasta, ¼ lb (125 g)

Salt and freshly ground pepper

Fresh flat-leaf (Italian) parsley, 3 tablespoons chopped

SERVES 4

egg noodles with roasted squash

Butternut or calabaza squash, 1 lb (500 g), peeled, seeded, and cut into small cubes

Salt and freshly ground pepper

Unsalted butter, 7 tablespoons (3 ½ oz/105 g), at room temperature

Olive oil, 1 tablespoon

Fresh sage, 8 large leaves

Pine nuts, ⅓ cup (2 oz/ 60 g), lightly toasted and coarsely chopped

Heavy (double) cream, ½ cup (4 fl oz/125 ml)

Wide egg noodles or pappardelle, 1 lb (500 g)

SERVES 4

1 **Roast the squash**
Preheat the oven to 450°F (230°C). Lightly oil a baking sheet. Arrange the squash cubes on the sheet in a single layer and season lightly with salt and pepper. Roast until golden brown and tender, 15–25 minutes. Set aside.

2 **Make the sauce**
Meanwhile, bring a large pot of water to a boil. In a large frying pan over medium-low heat, melt the butter with the oil. Add the sage and sauté until fragrant, about 4 minutes. Add the pine nuts and cream, stir to combine, and remove from the heat. Remove the sage and discard. Season to taste with salt and pepper.

3 **Cook the pasta**
Add 2 tablespoons salt and the pasta to the boiling water. Cook, stirring occasionally to prevent sticking, until al dente, according to the package directions. Drain, reserving about ½ cup (4 fl oz/125 ml) of the cooking water. Add the pasta to the sauce. Add the roasted squash and stir to combine. Add as much of the cooking water as needed to loosen the sauce and serve.

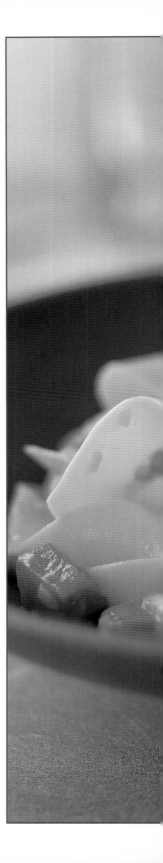

cook's tip

To prepare a winter squash, first cut it in half lengthwise with a sharp knife. Then use a vegetable peeler to remove the thin outer layer. Scoop out the seeds with a large metal spoon and cut the flesh into bite-sized pieces.

country-style
pasta & bean soup

1 Make the soup

In a large pot over low heat, warm the oil. Add the onion and sauté until fragrant but not colored, about 2 minutes. Raise the heat to medium and add the carrot, garlic, bay leaves, and sausage. Cook, stirring occasionally, until the vegetables are softened and the sausage is lightly browned, about 5 minutes. Reduce the heat to medium-low, cover, and cook, stirring occasionally, about 3 minutes. Stir in the beans and the tomato paste. Add the broth and bring to a simmer. Reduce the heat to low, partially cover, and cook, stirring occasionally, until the flavors come together, about 15 minutes.

2 Cook the pasta

Add the pasta to the soup and cook, stirring often, until the pasta is not quite al dente, about 2 minutes less than the package directions. The pasta will continue to cook in the heat of the soup. Add the parsley. Remove the bay leaves and discard. Season to taste with salt and pepper and serve.

Olive oil, 5 tablespoons (2½ fl oz/75 ml)

Yellow onion, 1 small, chopped

Carrot, 1 small, chopped

Garlic, 2 large cloves, minced

Bay leaves, 2

Smoked sausage, such as luganega, linguiça, or kielbasa, ½ lb (250 g), cut into small pieces

Canned pink or pinto beans, 4 cups (28 oz/875 g), drained and rinsed

Tomato paste, 1 tablespoon

Chicken broth, 9 cups (72 fl oz/2.2 l)

Tubetti, macaroni, or other small tubular pasta, ¼ lb (125 g)

Fresh flat-leaf (Italian) parsley, 3 tablespoons minced

Salt and freshly ground pepper

SERVES 6

penne with pork & peppers

Pork tenderloin, 1 ½ lb (750 g), thinly sliced against the grain, then cut into thin strips

Salt and freshly ground pepper

Olive oil, 6 tablespoons (3 fl oz/90 ml)

Yellow onion, 1 large, halved and thinly sliced

Red and yellow bell peppers (capsicums), 3 large, stems and seeds removed, cut into thin strips

Garlic, 2 large cloves, minced

Dry white wine, ½ cup (4 fl oz/125 ml)

Fresh marjoram, ½ teaspoon minced

Ground fennel seed, ½ teaspoon

Chicken broth, ¾ cup (6 fl oz/180 ml)

Penne, farfalle, or other medium-sized pasta, ¾ lb (375 g)

SERVES 4

1 Make the sauce

Bring a large pot of water to a boil. Season the pork with salt and pepper. In a deep frying pan over medium-low heat, warm 3 tablespoons of the oil. Add the onion, peppers, and garlic and sauté until the onion is lightly golden, about 4 minutes. Raise the heat to high, add the pork, and cook, turning occasionally, until nicely browned, 6–7 minutes. Reduce the heat to medium, add the wine, and cook until most of the alcohol has evaporated, about 1 minute. Add the marjoram, ground fennel seed, and broth. Cover and simmer, stirring occasionally, until the meat is tender, 10–12 minutes. Season with ¾ teaspoon salt and ½ teaspoon pepper.

2 Cook the pasta

Meanwhile, add 2 tablespoons salt and the pasta to the boiling water. Cook, stirring occasionally to prevent sticking, until al dente, according to the package directions. Drain, reserving about ½ cup (4 fl oz/125 ml) of the cooking water. Add the pasta to the sauce and stir to combine. Add as much of the cooking water as needed to loosen the sauce and serve.

cook's tip

The easiest way to cut meat such as pork tenderloin very thinly is to partially freeze the meat by placing it in the freezer for 30 minutes before slicing. The knife will glide through with much less resistance, allowing you to slice the meat almost paper thin.

cook's tip

When you roast garlic, include another head or two to save for other uses. Squeeze the roasted garlic from the cloves and store in an airtight container. It will keep in the refrigerator for up to 3 days or in the freezer for up to 3 months.

farfalle with roasted garlic & eggplant

1 Roast the eggplant and garlic

Preheat the oven to 400°F (200°C). Brush both sides of the eggplant slices lightly with 2 tablespoons of the oil and season with salt and pepper. Cut the garlic head in half crosswise and drizzle both halves with another 2 tablespoons of the oil. Place the eggplant and the garlic on 2 baking sheets, making sure the eggplant slices are not touching. Roast until the eggplant slices are nicely browned, 20–25 minutes. Remove from the oven and let cool. Continue to roast the garlic until soft and fragrant, about 20 minutes longer. Cut the eggplant slices into small pieces.

2 Make the sauce

Bring a large pot of water to a boil. Squeeze the garlic pulp from the cloves. In a large serving bowl, combine the remaining 4 tablespoons oil and the garlic, mashing and blending well. Stir in the tomatoes, basil, ½ teaspoon salt, and pepper to taste.

3 Cook the pasta

Meanwhile, add 2 tablespoons salt and the pasta to the boiling water. Cook, stirring occasionally to prevent sticking, until al dente, according to the package directions. Drain, reserving about ½ cup (4 fl oz/125 ml) of the cooking water. Add the pasta to the sauce along with the roasted eggplant and the mozzarella. Toss to combine. Add as much of the cooking water as needed to loosen the sauce and serve.

Eggplants (aubergines), 2 small, 1½ lb (750 g) total weight, cut crosswise into ½-inch (12-mm) slices

Olive oil, 8 tablespoons (4 fl oz/125 ml)

Salt and freshly ground pepper

Garlic, 1 head

Cherry tomatoes, 1 lb (500 g), halved

Fresh basil, ½ cup (¾ oz/20 g) minced

Farfalle, rigatoni, or other medium-sized pasta, 1 lb (500 g)

Fresh mozzarella cheese, 3 oz (90 g), cut into small pieces

SERVES 4

spaghetti alla puttanesca

Olive oil, ¼ cup
(2 fl oz/60 ml)

Garlic, 3 large cloves, minced

Anchovy fillets in olive oil,
3, chopped, plus 1 tablespoon
of the oil

**Canned whole plum
(Roma) tomatoes,** 2½ cups
(20 fl oz/625 ml) chopped,
with juice

Pitted black olives, ¼ cup
(1½ oz/45 g) chopped

Capers, ¼ cup (2 oz/60 g)

Fresh oregano, 1 teaspoon
minced

Fresh thyme, 1 teaspoon
minced

Red pepper flakes,
½ teaspoon

Salt

**Spaghetti or other strand
pasta,** 1 lb (500 g)

**Fresh flat-leaf (Italian)
parsley,** 3 tablespoons
minced

SERVES 4

1 Make the sauce
Bring a large pot of water to a boil. In a large frying pan over low heat, warm the oil and garlic until fragrant but not colored, about 2 minutes. Add the anchovies and their oil and cook, mashing them with a wooden spoon, for about 2 minutes. Raise the heat to medium and add the tomatoes and their juice, and the olives, capers, oregano, thyme, and red pepper flakes. Cook, stirring frequently, until the sauce thickens, about 20 minutes. Season to taste with salt.

2 Cook the pasta
Meanwhile, add 2 tablespoons salt and the pasta to the boiling water. Cook, stirring occasionally to prevent sticking, until al dente, according to the package directions. Drain, reserving about ½ cup (4 fl oz/125 ml) of the cooking water. Add the pasta to the sauce along with the parsley, tossing to combine. Add as much of the cooking water as needed to loosen the sauce. Warm briefly over low heat to blend the flavors and serve.

cook's tip

Because this sauce keeps well, you can double the recipe and use half of the sauce for tonight's dinner. Store the remaining sauce in an airtight container for up to 3 days in the refrigerator or for up to 3 months in the freezer.

penne with spring vegetables

1 Blanch the asparagus

Bring a large pot of water to a boil. Add 2 tablespoons salt and the asparagus to the boiling water and cook until tender, about 4 minutes. Using a skimmer or slotted spoon, transfer to a colander to drain; set aside. Return the water to a boil.

2 Make the sauce

In a large frying pan over medium-low heat, melt the butter with the oil. Add the green onions and sauté until wilted, about 5 minutes. Stir in the spinach and the peas and sauté until the spinach is wilted, about 3 minutes. Add the blanched asparagus, stir in the wine, and cook until most of the alcohol has evaporated, about 1 minute. Stir in the cream and cook until heated through. Add the basil and season to taste with salt and pepper.

3 Finish the dish

Meanwhile, add the pasta to the boiling water. Cook, stirring occasionally to prevent sticking, until al dente, according to the package directions. Drain, reserving about ½ cup (4 fl oz/ 125 ml) of the cooking water. Add the pasta to the sauce and toss to combine. Add as much of the cooking water as needed to loosen the sauce. Warm briefly over low heat to blend the flavors. Serve, passing the Parmesan at the table.

Salt and freshly ground pepper

Asparagus, ¾ lb (750 g), trimmed and cut into 1-inch (2.5-cm) pieces

Unsalted butter, 3 tablespoons

Olive oil, 3 tablespoons

Green (spring) onions, 3 bunches, white and pale green parts, thinly sliced

Baby spinach, 6 oz (185 g), coarsely chopped

Frozen petite peas, ½ lb (250 g)

Dry white wine, ½ cup (4 fl oz/125 ml)

Heavy (double) cream, ½ cup (4 fl oz/250 ml)

Fresh basil, ½ cup (¾ oz/20 g) minced

Penne or other medium-sized pasta, 1 lb (500 g)

Parmesan cheese, ½ cup (2 oz/60 g) freshly grated

SERVES 4

cavatelli with chicken & tomato

Unsalted butter, 2 tablespoons

Olive oil, 3 tablespoons

Chicken thighs and drumsticks, 3 lb (1.5 kg)

Chicken livers, ½ lb (8 oz/250 g), cleaned, trimmed of fat, and coarsely chopped (optional)

Yellow onion, 1 small, finely chopped

Carrot, 1, finely chopped

Celery, 1 stalk, finely chopped

Bay leaves, 2

Cremini or button mushrooms, ¼ lb (125 g), quartered and thinly sliced

Canned crushed plum (Roma) tomatoes, 2½ cups (20 fl oz/625 ml) with juice

Salt and freshly ground pepper

Cavatelli, fusilli, or other medium-sized pasta, 1 lb (500 g)

SERVES 6

1 Brown the chicken
In a large frying pan over medium-high heat, melt the butter with 1 tablespoon of the oil. Working in batches, add the chicken to the pan and cook, turning once, until brown on both sides, about 10 minutes total per batch. Remove from the pan and set aside. In the same pan, warm 1 tablespoon of the oil. Add the livers, if using, and cook, stirring frequently, until browned, about 5 minutes. Transfer to a plate and set aside.

2 Make the sauce
Return the pan to medium heat and warm the remaining 1 tablespoon oil. Add the onion, carrot, celery, and bay leaves and sauté until the vegetables are softened and slightly browned, about 7 minutes. Add the mushrooms and sauté until they have released some of their liquid, about 3 minutes. Stir in the tomatoes. Add the chicken along with the liver (if using) and any accumulated juices. Reduce the heat to low and simmer, partially covered, until the chicken is opaque throughout, about 30 minutes. Remove the bay leaves and discard. Season to taste with salt and pepper.

3 Cook the pasta
Meanwhile, bring a large pot of water to a boil. Add 2 tablespoons salt and the pasta. Cook, stirring occasionally to prevent sticking, until al dente, according to the package directions. Drain and divide among bowls. Top with the sauce and chicken pieces, and serve.

cook's tip

To make this recipe faster, use a
purchased rotisserie chicken. Cut
it into 6 pieces. Prepare the sauce
as directed in step 2, simmering
the chicken pieces in the sauce
for about 15 minutes while you
cook the pasta.

cook's tip

Instead of using pancetta, ask
your butcher or delicatessen for
prosciutto ends. The cost should
be a fraction of the price of
sliced prosciutto.

lentil soup
with pasta

1 Make the soup base
In a large pot over medium-high heat, warm the oil. Add the pancetta and sauté until lightly browned, about 2 minutes. Add the onion, garlic, carrot, celery, and sage and sauté until the vegetables are softened, about 3 minutes.

2 Cook the lentils
Stir in the lentils and tomatoes and cook, stirring occasionally, for 5 minutes. Raise the heat to high, add the broth, and bring to a boil. Add 1 tablespoon salt, reduce the heat to medium-low, and simmer, partially covered, until the lentils are nearly tender, 30–40 minutes. Add more broth if the soup starts to dry out.

3 Cook the pasta
Add the pasta to the lentils. Cook, stirring occasionally to prevent sticking, until the pasta is not quite al dente, about 2 minutes less than the package directions. The pasta will continue to cook in the heat of the soup. Season to taste with salt and pepper. Ladle the soup into bowls and serve.

Olive oil, 3 tablespoons

Pancetta or bacon, 2 oz (60 g), chopped

Yellow onion, 1 small, chopped

Garlic, 2 large cloves, minced

Carrot, 1, finely chopped

Celery, 1 stalk, finely chopped

Fresh sage, 1 tablespoon, minced

Lentils, 2 cups (14 oz/440 g)

Canned whole plum (Roma) tomatoes, 1 cup (8 fl oz/250 ml), chopped, with juice

Chicken broth, 6 cups (48 fl oz/1.5 l), plus more if needed

Salt and freshly ground pepper

Tubettini, ditalini, or other small soup pasta, ¼ lb (125 g)

SERVES 4

penne with beef ragù

Olive oil, 6 tablespoons
(3 fl oz/90 ml)

Yellow onion, 1 small,
finely chopped

Garlic, 3 large cloves, minced

Carrot, 1, finely chopped

Celery, 1 stalk, finely chopped

Fresh rosemary, 1 teaspoon
minced

Ground (minced) beef,
¾ lb (375 g)

Dry red wine, ½ cup
(4 fl oz/125 ml)

Tomato paste, 3 tablespoons

**Canned whole plum
(Roma) tomatoes,** 2½ cups
(20 fl oz/625 ml), chopped,
with juice

**Salt and freshly ground
pepper**

Penne or rigatoni,
1 lb (500 g)

SERVES 4

1 Make the sauce
In a large, deep frying pan or Dutch oven over medium-low heat, warm the olive oil. Add the onion, garlic, carrot, celery, and rosemary and sauté until the vegetables are softened, about 8 minutes. Add 1–2 tablespoons water if necessary to keep the pan from drying out and the vegetables from browning. Add the meat and cook, breaking it up with a wooden spoon, until it is browned, about 10 minutes. Add the wine and the tomato paste. Cook, stirring occasionally, until most of the alcohol has evaporated, about 4 minutes. Reduce the heat to low and add the tomatoes, 1 teaspoon salt, and ½ teaspoon pepper. Cover partially and cook, stirring occasionally, until the sauce is thick and aromatic, about 1 hour.

2 Cook the pasta
Meanwhile, bring a large pot of water to a boil. Add 2 tablespoons salt and the pasta. Cook, stirring occasionally to prevent sticking, until al dente, according to the package directions. Drain and add to the sauce, stirring to combine. Warm briefly over low heat to blend the flavors. Season to taste with salt and pepper and serve.

cook's tip

Ragù—which can be made with ground (minced) beef, pork, veal, or a combination—tastes even better the day after it is made. This recipe can easily be doubled and will keep in an airtight container for up to 3 days in the refrigerator or for up to 3 months in the freezer.

make more
to store

fusilli with tomato-basil sauce

TOMATO-BASIL SAUCE

Olive oil, ¼ cup (2 fl oz/ 60 ml)

Garlic, 4 large cloves, minced

Tomato paste, ½ cup (4 oz/125 g)

Canned whole plum (Roma) tomatoes, 8 cups (64 fl oz/2 l), chopped, with juice

Fresh basil, 10–12 leaves

Salt and freshly ground pepper

Fusilli, penne, or other medium-sized pasta, 1 lb (500 g)

Parmesan cheese, ½ cup (2 oz/60 g) freshly grated

SERVES 4

makes 8 cups (64 fl oz/2 l) sauce total

This basic tomato sauce pairs perfectly with almost every pasta shape, from farfalle to ziti. The recipe makes enough tomato sauce for dinner tonight plus the following two recipes.

1 **Make the sauce**
Bring a large pot of water to a boil. In a large saucepan over medium-low heat, warm the oil. Add the garlic and sauté until lightly golden, about 3 minutes. Stir in the tomato paste. Add the tomatoes, the basil, and ½ teaspoon salt. Bring to a simmer and cook, stirring occasionally, until the tomatoes break down, about 15 minutes. Remove from the heat and let cool slightly. Using a food processor or immersion blender, process the sauce until smooth. Or, position a food mill with the fine shredding disk over a large saucepan and pass the sauce through it. Season the sauce with salt and pepper.

2 **Cook the pasta**
Meanwhile, add 2 tablespoons salt and the pasta to the boiling water. Cook, stirring occasionally to prevent sticking, until al dente, according to the package directions. Place 2 cups (16 fl oz/500 ml) of the sauce in a warmed serving bowl. Drain the pasta and toss with the sauce. Serve, passing the Parmesan at the table.

storage tip

The tomato-basil sauce can
be stored in airtight containers
in the refrigerator for up to
3 days or in the freezer for up
to 3 months. When reheating
the sauce, stir in an additional
1–2 tablespoons olive oil.

cook's tip

You can prepare the meatballs up to 2 months in advance. After forming the raw meatballs, place them on a baking sheet or other pan and freeze thoroughly, about 2 hours. Transfer to an airtight container. Before using, defrost the meatballs in the refrigerator overnight.

spaghetti & meatballs

1 Prepare the meatballs

In a small bowl, combine the bread cubes and milk. Let stand about 3 minutes, then squeeze the bread dry, discarding the milk. In a bowl, combine the softened bread, beef, onion, parsley, thyme, egg, ¼ cup (1 oz/30 g) of the Parmesan, 1 teaspoon salt, and ½ teaspoon pepper. Mix gently with your hands. Form into balls about 1 inch (2.5 cm) in diameter.

2 Cook the meatballs

In a large frying pan over medium heat, pour oil to a depth of ½ inch (12 mm). When the oil is hot, add the meatballs, in batches if necessary, and cook, turning occasionally, until browned on all sides, about 12 minutes. Transfer to a plate lined with paper towels to drain. Discard the oil and place the pan over medium-low heat. Pour the tomato-basil sauce into the pan, stirring and scraping up any browned bits from the pan bottom. Add the meatballs and cook, covered, until cooked through, about 15 minutes.

3 Cook the pasta

Meanwhile, bring a large pot of water to a boil. Add 2 tablespoons salt and the pasta. Cook, stirring occasionally to prevent sticking, until al dente, according to the package directions. Drain and add to the sauce. Gently toss to combine. Transfer to a large bowl and serve. Pass the remaining Parmesan at the table.

Tomato-Basil Sauce, 2½ cups (20 fl oz/625 ml), homemade (page 76) or purchased

---

Day-old coarse country bread, crusts removed, ¾ cup (¾ oz/20 g) cubed

Milk, ⅓ cup (3 fl oz/80 ml)

Ground (minced) beef, 1 lb (500 g)

Yellow onion, 1 small, shredded

Fresh flat-leaf (Italian) parsley, 2 tablespoons minced

Fresh thyme, 1 teaspoon minced

Egg, 1, beaten

Parmesan cheese, ¾ cup (3 oz/90 g) freshly grated

Salt and freshly ground pepper

Olive oil for frying

Spaghetti, 1 lb (500 g)

SERVES 6

sausage lasagna

Tomato-Basil Sauce,
2½ cups (20 fl oz/625 ml),
homemade (page 76)
or purchased

Olive oil, 1 tablespoon

Sweet Italian sausage,
1½ lb (750 g), casings
removed and crumbled

Fresh ricotta, 2 cups
(1 lb/500 g)

Milk, ¼ cup (2 fl oz/60 ml)

Nutmeg, ⅛ teaspoon freshly
grated

No-cook lasagna noodles,
1 lb (500 g)

Mozzarella cheese,
½ lb (250 g), shredded

Parmesan cheese, ½ cup
(2 oz/60 g) freshly grated

SERVES 6

1 Cook the sausage
Preheat the oven to 400°F (200°C). In a frying pan over medium heat, warm the oil. Add the sausage and sauté, stirring occasionally, until browned, about 10 minutes. Transfer the sausage to a plate and set aside.

2 Assemble the lasagna
In a bowl, stir together the ricotta, milk, and nutmeg. Spread about ¼ cup (2 fl oz/60 ml) of the tomato-basil sauce on the bottom of a 10-by-12-by-2-inch (25-by-30-by-5-cm) baking dish. Cover with a single layer of lasagna noodles without overlapping them. Spread with one-third of the remaining sauce, followed by half of the ricotta mixture, and one-third of the sausage. Add another layer of noodles, top with one-third of the sauce, the remaining half of the ricotta mixture, and one-third of the sausage. Top with another layer of noodles and the remaining sauce and sausage, and then cover with an even layer of mozzarella and Parmesan.

3 Bake the lasagna
Cover the dish with aluminum foil and bake for 45 minutes. Remove the foil and continue baking until the noodles are tender and the cheese is golden and bubbly, about 10 minutes longer. Remove from the oven and let stand for 10 minutes. Cut into squares and serve.

cook's tip

No-boil lasagna noodles, which
do not need to be precooked,
are widely available. Layer these
dried pasta sheets as you would
boiled pasta. The no-cook
noodles will absorb liquid and
cook during baking.

bucatini
with pesto

PESTO SAUCE

Fresh basil, 4 cups (4 oz/ 125 g) tightly packed

Garlic, 4 large cloves, minced

Olive oil, 1 cup (8 fl oz/ 250 ml)

Pine nuts, ⅔ cup (3 oz/ 90 g), lightly toasted

Salt and freshly ground pepper

Parmesan or pecorino romano cheese, or a combination, 1½ cups (6 oz/180 g) freshly grated, plus ½ cup (2 oz/60 g) for serving

Unsalted butter, 4 tablespoons (2 oz/60 g), at room temperature

Bucatini, spaghetti, or other strand pasta, 1 lb (500 g)

SERVES 4

makes 5 cups (40 fl oz/ 1.25 l) sauce total

Pesto is one of the easiest sauces to make, as it requires no cooking, just a quick combining of fresh ingredients. This recipe makes enough pesto for dinner tonight plus the following two recipes.

1 Make the pesto
Bring a large pot of water to a boil. In the bowl of a food processor, combine the basil, garlic, oil, and pine nuts, 1 teaspoon salt, and several grindings of pepper. Process until a coarse paste forms, stopping occasionally to scrape down the sides of the bowl with a rubber spatula. Transfer to a bowl and stir in the 1½ cups grated cheese and the butter.

2 Cook the pasta
Add 2 tablespoons salt and the pasta to the boiling water. Cook, stirring occasionally to prevent sticking, until al dente, according to the package directions. Drain, reserving about ½ cup (4 fl oz/125 ml) of the cooking water. In a serving bowl, mix 2 tablespoons of the cooking water with 1 cup (8 fl oz/250 ml) of the pesto. Add the drained pasta and toss to combine. Add as much of the remaining cooking water as needed to loosen the sauce. Serve, passing the remaining ½ cup grated cheese at the table.

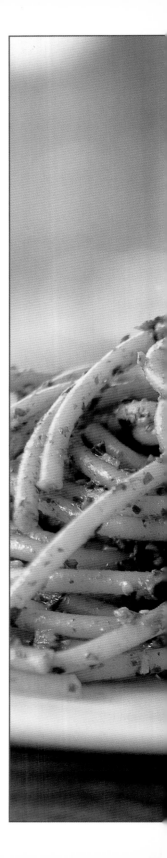

storage tip

The pesto sauce can be stored in an airtight container in the refrigerator for up to 2 days or in the freezer for up to 2 months. Press a piece of plastic wrap on the surface of the pesto before storing to prevent discoloring.

cook's tip

The green beans and potatoes
can be cooked 1 day in advance.
Leave the potatoes whole, and
peel and chop them just before
using. Add the potatoes and
green beans to the boiling pasta
1 minute before the pasta is
al dente, to heat them through.
Drain the pasta and vegetables,
and then toss with the pesto
as directed.

ziti with pesto & potatoes

1 Cook the potatoes

Put the potatoes in a saucepan with cold water to cover. Bring to a boil over high heat, reduce the heat to medium, and cook until tender when pierced with a sharp knife, about 20 minutes. Drain the potatoes. When they are cool enough to handle, remove the skins and cut the potatoes into cubes.

2 Cook the pasta and green beans

Meanwhile, bring a large pot of water to a boil. Add 2 tablespoons salt and the pasta. Cook, stirring occasionally to prevent sticking, until al dente, according to the package directions. Add the beans to the boiling water about 5 minutes before the pasta is ready.

3 Finish the dish

Drain the pasta and beans, reserving about ½ cup (4 fl oz/125 ml) of the cooking water. In a serving bowl, mix a few tablespoons of the cooking water with the pesto. Add the potatoes. Add the pasta and beans and toss to combine. Add as much of the remaining cooking water as needed to loosen the sauce. Serve, passing the Parmesan at the table.

Pesto Sauce, 1 cup (8 fl oz/ 250 ml), homemade (page 82) or purchased

White boiling potatoes, 3, about 5 oz (155 g) total weight

Salt

Ziti, penne, or other tubular pasta, ¾ lb (375 g)

Green beans, about ⅓ lb (5 oz/155 g), trimmed and cut crosswise into thirds

Parmesan cheese, ½ cup (2 oz/60 g) freshly grated

SERVES 4

85

minestrone with pasta & pesto

Pesto Sauce, 1 cup (8 fl oz/
250 ml), homemade (page 82)
or purchased

Olive oil, 5 tablespoons
(2½ fl oz/75 ml)

Yellow onion, 1, chopped

Chicken broth, 7 cups
(56 fl oz/1.75 l)

Green cabbage, 1 head,
shredded

**Canned whole plum (Roma)
tomatoes,** 1 cup (8 fl oz/
250 ml), chopped, with juice

Carrot, 1, finely chopped

Rutabaga, 1, chopped

**Salt and freshly ground
pepper**

**Chickpeas (garbanzo
beans),** 1 can (14 oz/440 g),
drained and rinsed

Zucchini (courgettes),
2 small, chopped

**Conchigliette, ditalini,
or other small soup pasta,**
1 cup (3½ oz/105 g)

Parmesan cheese, ¼ cup
(1 oz/30 g) freshly grated

SERVES 8

1 Make the soup

In a large pot over medium-low heat, warm the oil. Add the onion and sauté until softened, about 5 minutes. Add the broth, cabbage, tomatoes, carrot, and rutabaga. Season with 1 teaspoon salt and ½ teaspoon pepper. Raise the heat to high, cover, and bring to a boil. Reduce the heat to medium-low and cook, partially covered, until the vegetables are tender, about 30 minutes.

2 Finish the soup

Stir in the chickpeas and zucchini, and simmer, partially covered, for 5 minutes. Raise the heat to medium and add the pasta. Cook, uncovered and stirring often, until the pasta is al dente, about 5 minutes. Taste and adjust the seasoning with salt and pepper. Ladle the soup into bowls and stir a spoonful of the pesto into each serving. Top with the cheese and serve.

cook's tip

A variety of vegetables can be used in minestrone. If you like, add 1 cup (4 oz/125 g) chopped celery or the same amount of chopped cauliflower instead of the rutabaga and cabbage.

rigatoni with pork ragù

PORK RAGÙ

Olive oil, ½ cup (4 fl oz/ 125 ml)

Yellow onion, 1 large, finely chopped

Carrots, 2, finely chopped

Celery, 2 stalks, finely chopped

Ground fennel seed, 2 teaspoons

Ground (minced) pork, 1 lb (500 g)

Dry red wine, 1 cup (8 fl oz/250 ml)

Canned whole plum (Roma) tomatoes, 4 cups (32 fl oz/1 l), chopped, with juice

Tomato paste, ¼ cup (2 oz/60 g)

Salt

Rigatoni or other large pasta shape, 1 lb (500 g)

Parmesan cheese, ½ cup (2 oz/60 g) freshly grated

SERVES 4

makes 8 cups (64 fl oz/2 l) sauce total

This rich sauce, redolent of red wine and the sweet flavors of pork and fennel, is a classic pairing with rigatoni. This recipe makes enough sauce for dinner tonight plus the following two recipes.

1 Make the sauce
In a Dutch oven or other heavy pot over medium heat, warm the oil. Add the onion, carrots, and celery and sauté until softened, about 10 minutes. Add the ground fennel seed and pork and cook, breaking up the meat with a wooden spoon, until the meat colors slightly, about 4 minutes. Stir in the wine and cook until most of the alcohol has evaporated, 1–2 minutes. Add the tomatoes, the tomato paste, and ½ teaspoon salt. Stir well to combine. Reduce the heat to low and simmer, partially covered and stirring occasionally, until the sauce has thickened and the flavors have melded, about 1 hour. If the sauce seems to be drying out, add a few tablespoons of water.

2 Cook the pasta
Meanwhile, bring a large pot of water to a boil. Add 2 tablespoons salt and the pasta. Cook, stirring occasionally, until al dente, according to the package directions. Place 2 cups (16 fl oz/500 ml) of the sauce in a warmed serving bowl. Drain the pasta and add to the sauce, stirring to coat. Serve, passing the Parmesan at the table.

storage tip

The pork ragù can be made in advance and stored in an airtight container for up to 3 days in the refrigerator or for up to 3 months in the freezer.

cook's tip

You can roast the eggplant up to 1 day in advance. Store in an airtight container or a resealable plastic bag in the refrigerator. Select young eggplants with taut skin and even coloring.

baked ziti
with pork ragù

1 Roast the eggplant

Preheat the oven to 450°F (230°C). Line 2 baking sheets with parchment (baking) paper or aluminum foil. In a small bowl, combine the oil and ½ teaspoon each salt and pepper. Drizzle the eggplant chunks with the oil mixture and arrange on the prepared sheets so they are not touching. Roast until golden, about 10 minutes. Remove from the oven and let cool. Reduce the oven temperature to 400°F (200°C).

2 Cook the pasta

Meanwhile, bring a large pot of water to a boil. Add 2 tablespoons salt and the pasta. Cook, stirring occasionally to prevent sticking, until still very al dente, about half of the timing on the package directions. Drain and rinse under running cold water to stop the cooking; drain well again.

3 Assemble and bake the dish

In a large bowl, toss together the pasta, ragù, roasted eggplant, and tomatoes. Spread half of the ragù mixture on the bottom of a 9-by-12-by-2-inch (23-by-30-by-5-cm) or 1½ qt (1.5 l) baking dish. Combine the two cheeses and sprinkle half the mixture over the ragù mixture in the dish. Cover with the remaining ragù mixture and sprinkle with the remaining cheese. Cover with foil and bake for 20 minutes. Remove the foil and bake until the surface is golden and bubbly, about 5 minutes longer. Let cool for 10 minutes before serving.

Pork Ragù, 2 cups (16 fl oz/ 500 ml), homemade (page 88) or purchased

Olive oil, 6 tablespoons (3 fl oz/90 ml)

Salt and freshly ground pepper

Eggplants (aubergines), 3 small, cut into chunks

Ziti, penne, or other tubular pasta, ¾ lb (375 g)

Tomatoes, 2, chopped

Fresh mozzarella cheese, ½ lb (250 g), cut into small pieces

Parmesan cheese, ½ cup (2 oz/60 g) freshly grated

SERVES 6

91

stuffed shells with pork ragù

Pork Ragù, 2½ cups (20 fl oz/ 625 ml), homemade (page 88) or purchased

Salt and freshly ground pepper

Conchiglioni or other large pasta shells, ½ lb (250 g)

Fresh ricotta cheese, 2 lb (1 kg)

Egg yolks, 2, lightly beaten

Parmesan cheese, 1½ cups (6 oz/185 g) freshly grated

Nutmeg, ¼ teaspoon freshly grated

SERVES 8

1 Cook the pasta

Bring a large pot of water to a boil. Add 2 tablespoons salt and the pasta. Cook, stirring occasionally to prevent sticking, until still very al dente, about 3 minutes less than the package directions. Drain and rinse under running cold water to stop the cooking; drain well and set aside.

2 Prepare the filling

Preheat the oven to 375°F (190°C). In a bowl, combine the ricotta, the egg yolks, 1 cup (4 oz/125 g) of the Parmesan, the nutmeg, 1 teaspoon salt, and ½ teaspoon pepper.

3 Stuff and bake the shells

Spread 2–3 tablespoons ragù on the bottom of a 9-by-12-inch (23-by-30-cm) baking dish. Using a teaspoon, stuff the pasta shells with the filling. Do not overstuff the shells. Place the stuffed shells in the dish and top with the remaining sauce. Sprinkle with the remaining ½ cup (2 oz/60 g) Parmesan and cover with aluminum foil. Bake for 15 minutes. Remove the foil and bake until golden and bubbly, 10 minutes longer. Remove from the oven and let stand for 10 minutes before serving.

cook's tip

To stuff the pasta shells neatly and easily, put the ricotta filling in a plastic bag. Work the filling into the bottom of the bag and twist the top of the bag to close. Snip off one corner of the bag and squeeze the filling into the shells.

the smarter cook

Having a collection of easy pasta recipes on hand is the starting point for getting dinner on the table quickly, especially during the week when time is limited. Combine them with a few simple strategies—knowing what's in your pantry, putting together a weekly meal plan, cooking extra sauce to store—and you'll be able to whip up a wonderful pasta meal in record time any night of the week.

Keep your pantry well stocked, and you have the foundation for all your weeknight suppers. Plan your meals, and you'll make fewer trips to the store. Cook up a big batch of sauce when you have extra time; serve some for dinner tonight and use the rest in multiple recipes throughout the week. In the following pages, you'll find tips on how to manage your time and stock your kitchen—the keys to becoming a smarter cook.

get started

With a little planning and a well-organized kitchen, you can become a smarter cook who regularly turns out delicious pasta dishes with ease and speed. Three simple strategies will make it possible: drawing up a weekly meal plan, figuring out when to fit cooking into your busy schedule, and keeping your pantry and refrigerator stocked with basic items (pages 104–107).

plan a pasta meal

Get into the habit of putting together a weekly meal plan, which can take the worry out of what to cook for dinner and provide make-ahead opportunities that will save you time when you need it most. See the sample meals to the right for ideas. Once you have settled on your meals, you can create a list of the fresh ingredients you need to make the recipes, which you can then pick up in a few efficient shopping trips.

- **Pasta is versatile.** Think of pasta as a healthy and delicious foundation for many flavor combinations, from sautéed vegetables and simmered seafood to spicy tomato sauces and hearty meat ragù. For variety, alternate serving meat- or vegetable-based pasta sauces with pasta soups and cream-sauced pastas.

- **Pasta can be a first course or a main course.** Serve a pasta dish as a first course before meat or fish in the traditional Italian way, or offer it as a main course accompanied by a salad or vegetables for a lighter meal.

- **Plan seasonally.** Choose recipes that call for the fresh produce and other ingredients of the season, such as asparagus in the spring, tomatoes and zucchini in the summer, and butternut squash in the autumn and winter. Plan dishes that match the weather: hearty soups and robust meat sauces in the cool months, pesto or light vegetable and herb sauces in summer, and light soups and seasonal vegetable sauces in spring.

- **Stock a selection of pasta shapes.** Add variety to your menu by stocking pasta cuts that work with different types of sauces and soups, such as short, stubby shapes; ribbon and strand varieties; and soup pasta.

ROUND IT OUT

salad Dress salad greens or blanched fresh vegetables with a simple vinaigrette and serve before, alongside, or after the pasta. Harmonize the salad with the pasta dish. For example, serve a simple green salad with a sturdy pasta with cream sauce. Or, toss green beans with lemon juice and fruity olive oil and serve with pasta with a tomato sauce.

meats Arrange sliced cured meats, such as prosciutto, mortadella, or salami, on a plate and serve with the pasta. Or, grill sweet Italian sausages and serve with pasta tossed with a vegetable sauce.

cheeses If you are not serving pasta with a cheese sauce, offer a variety of fresh and aged cheeses on a cheese board. Or, arrange sliced fresh mozzarella and ripe tomatoes, drizzle with olive oil, and serve as a first course or side dish.

artisanal bread Warm bread briefly in the oven, if desired, then slice and serve with butter or extra-virgin olive oil.

vegetables Drizzle sautéed, steamed, or roasted vegetables with olive oil or melted butter, then sprinkle with salt, pepper, and fresh herbs.

sample meals

IN MINUTES meals include easy recipes and accompaniments that can be put together quickly. FROM THE PANTRY meals maximize ingredients from your pantry, saving you a trip to the store. FIT FOR COMPANY meals include ideas for stress-free get-togethers, complete with a wine suggestion.

IN MINUTES	FROM THE PANTRY	FIT FOR COMPANY
Spaghetti alla Carbonara (page 10) Roasted asparagus Garlic crostini	**Spaghettini with Olive Pesto** (page 18) Rotisserie chicken	**Rigatoni with Mushroom Ragù** (page 17) Braised greens with balsamic vinegar *Syrah or Zinfandel*
Orecchiette with Broccoli Rabe (page 13) Mixed salad greens with balsamic vinaigrette	**Penne with Vodka Sauce** (page 26) Steamed English peas	**Tagliatelle with Crab & Tarragon** (page 22) Butter lettuce & grapefruit salad *Sauvignon Blanc*
Three-Cheese Macaroni (page 21) Broiled chicken sausages & zucchini	**Cappellini with Lemon, Garlic & Parsley** (page 30) Smoked salmon Toasted baguette slices	**Gemelli with Brown Butter & Asparagus** (page 42) Grilled flank steak with black pepper *Zinfandel*
Fusilli with Zucchini & Goat Cheese (page 25) Pan-seared salmon fillets with lemon wedges	**Spaghetti all'Amatriciana** (page 52) Sliced salami & mortadella Assorted cheeses	**Farfalle with Veal & Pine Nuts** (page 49) Arugula (rocket) & Parmesan salad with red wine vinaigrette *Pinot Noir*
Linguine with Clams (page 34) Mixed salad greens with citrus vinaigrette Crusty bread	**Pasta with Chickpeas** (page 55) Spinach salad with bacon & mustard vinaigrette	**Egg Noodles with Roasted Squash** (page 56) Sautéed zucchini matchsticks with shaved Parmesan Roasted garlic & sliced baguette *Cabernet Franc or Chardonnay*
Creamy Penne with Walnuts (page 45) Sautéed chard	**Spaghetti alla Puttanesca** (page 64) Broiled Italian fennel sausages Green beans with olive oil & lemon zest	

MATCHING SAUCES & PASTA

butter sauces	conchiglie, farfalle, tagliatelle
cheese sauces	bucatini, conchiglie, farfalle, fusilli, gemelli, macaroni
cream sauces	gemelli, pappardelle, penne, tagliatelle
oil-based sauces	capellini, farfalle, spaghetti, spaghettini
pesto	bucatini, linguine, penne
ragù & meat sauces	bucatini, conchiglie, fettuccine, fusilli, gemelli, linguine, orecchiette, pappardelle, penne, rigatoni, spaghetti, ziti
seafood sauces	linguine, spaghetti, spaghettini
tomato sauces	conchiglie, farfalle, linguine, penne, spaghetti, spaghettini, tagliatelle
vegetable sauces	cavatelli, gemelli, orecchiette, penne, rigatoni, ziti
broths & soups	small pasta shapes such as ditali, ditalini, orzo, tubetti
baked pastas	lasagna, penne, ziti

MATCHING CHEESE & PASTA

cheese for stuffing or layering pasta	fresh ricotta, mascarpone, mozzarella
cheese for sauces	fresh goat cheese, Gorgonzola, Gruyère
cheese for melting	Fontina, mozzarella, *scamorza*
hard cheese for grating	aged Asiago, aged pecorino, *grana padano,* Parmesan
semisoft cheese for grating	*ricotta salata,* young pecorino

PASTA SHAPES

bucatini	long, hollow strands
capellini	very thin, long strands
cavatelli	shells with rolled edges
conchiglie	shells
ditali	little thimbles
ditalini	tiny thimbles
farfalle	bow ties or butterflies
fettuccine	long ribbons
fusilli	twists
gemelli	twisted spiral tubes
lasagna	wide, flat noodles
linguine	long, flat strands
macaroni	elbows
orecchiette	little ears
orzo	barley-shaped pasta
pappardelle	long, wide ribbons
penne	tubes
penne rigate	ridged tubes
rigatoni	large, grooved tubes
spaghetti	long, round strands
spaghettini	long, thin round strands
tagliatelle	long, thin ribbons
tubetti	little tubes
ziti	long tubes

the dos and don'ts of perfect pasta

Cooking and serving perfect pasta every time is fast and easy if you follow these ten simple rules of preparation. Remember, you don't want to drown your pasta with sauce. Instead, toss it with sauce to coat evenly before plating.

DO use the finest-quality Italian dried pasta. Start with the best-quality imported Italian pasta, which retains its signature al dente character from the pot to the table. Find a good source, then purchase a few different shapes—long strands, short tubes, tiny soup pasta—to have on hand in your pantry.

DO boil pasta in plenty of water. To cook 1 lb (500 g) of pasta, fill a large pot no more than three-fourths full with about 5 qt (5 l) water. Cook pasta just before serving, never in advance. (Precooking pasta for lasagna and other baked dishes is an exception to the rule.)

DON'T add oil to the water. Contrary to popular belief, adding oil to the cooking water does not keep the pasta from sticking together. Instead it coats the pasta, which prevents the sauce from clinging to it.

DO add plenty of salt to the water. Once the water is boiling, add about 2 tablespoons kosher salt along with the pasta. If you are stingy with the salt, your pasta will have a blandness that no amount of salt added later can correct.

DO stir continually from the outset. Start stirring the pasta with a long spoon as soon as you drop it into the water, and continue to stir every minute or so to prevent it from sticking together.

DON'T overcook the pasta. Use the package directions as a guide to cooking time, but also check the pasta once or twice before the time has elapsed. It should be tender yet still slightly firm at the center.

DO save some cooking water. For many recipes, you need to scoop out and reserve about ½ cup (4 fl oz/ 125 ml) of the cooking water just before you drain the pasta. If the pasta still needs more moisture after saucing, add a little of the reserved water—usually no more than a few tablespoons—to bring the pasta and sauce together. Some sauces, such as pesto or unctuous cheese sauces, require more cooking water to thin them adequately and keep the pasta moist.

DO drain the pasta immediately. The moment the pasta is al dente, drain it right away to prevent it from cooking further. Use a sturdy, footed colander with plenty of good-sized holes, so that the water drains out as quickly as possible. Never rinse the drained pasta with water, or you'll remove some of the starch that helps the sauce adhere.

DO sauce the pasta immediately. If the sauce is hot, add the drained pasta directly to the sauce and toss or stir the two together over low heat for a few seconds, just until the pasta is coated, then remove from the heat and serve immediately. If you are serving an uncooked sauce, toss the pasta and sauce together in a large bowl before serving.

DON'T let the pasta cool off. Whether the sauce is hot or an uncooked cold sauce, such as pesto or some summer sauces, the pasta must always be steaming hot. To keep pasta from cooling immediately once it is served, warm the individual plates or shallow bowls for a few minutes in a 200°F (95°C) oven.

shop smarter

Using the best-quality ingredients is important to making simple meals delicious, so finding dependable sources is crucial. Seek out a butcher, a fishmonger, and markets that stock high-quality goods, and patronize them often. Call ahead and place your order, so it's ready to pick up on your way home from work. Visit farmers' markets regularly for the freshest produce and to keep up with what is in season.

■ **Pasta** Nothing beats the flavor and texture of imported Italian dried pasta. It has an elasticity that allows the pasta to stand up to cooking without becoming mushy. This ideal consistency—known as al dente—is essentially tender but firm. Good-quality pasta is a sunny color with tiny specks of wheat visible. As it cooks, it releases a nutty aroma and a wheaty flavor.

■ **Cheese** The best way to learn about artisanal cheeses is at good cheese shops where the sellers know their products. Examine both the labels and the cheeses carefully and, if possible, taste before you buy. Purchase cheeses in small quantities except when buying Parmesan. Genuine Parmesan (as opposed to other hard grating cheeses) will be labeled "Parmigiano-Reggiano" and will have a healthy straw color.

■ **Oil** Olive oil serves a dual purpose: it is both a cooking medium and a source of flavor. High-quality, cold-pressed extra-virgin olive oil, which imparts a unique flavor to sauces, is typically used in uncooked sauces or for drizzling over finished pasta dishes just before serving. Look for olive oil in dark glass bottles, as exposure to light shortens its life.

■ **Tomatoes** Thin-skinned, meaty plum (Roma) tomatoes make the best sauces; plus, their low water content means they cook faster. Good-quality canned tomatoes are an excellent alternative to out-of-season fresh tomatoes. Look for Italian San Marzano tomatoes for superior flavor.

■ **Produce** Buy organic produce whenever possible for better flavor and healthier eating. Greens and herbs should be crisp and brightly colored, and vegetables such as eggplants (aubergines) and zucchini (courgettes) should have taut skins and be firm to the touch. To save on prep time, purchase prewashed spinach or salad greens and broccoli crowns.

MAKE A SHOPPING LIST

prepare in advance Make a list of what you need to buy before you go shopping and you'll save time at the store.

make a template Create a list template on your computer, then fill it in during the week before you go shopping.

categorize your lists Use the following categories to keep your lists organized: pantry, fresh, and occasional.

■ **pantry items** Check the pantry and write down any items that need to be restocked to make the meals on your weekly plan.

■ **fresh ingredients** These are for immediate use and include produce, seafood, meats, and some cheeses. You might need to visit different stores or supermarket sections, so divide the list into subcategories, such as produce, dairy, and meats.

■ **occasional items** This is a revolving list for refrigerated items that are replaced as needed, such as butter and eggs.

be flexible Be ready to change your menus based on the freshest ingredients at the market.

PANTRY ITEMS

black pepper

bread crumbs

canned whole plum (Roma) tomatoes

chicken broth

dry white wine

garlic

olive oil

pasta: lasagna noodles, linguini,
macaroni, penne, rigatoni, spaghetti

red pepper flakes

salt

tomato paste

FRESH: PRODUCE

asparagus

basil

carrots

lemons

zucchini (courgettes)

FRESH: CHEESE

Gruyère

mozzarella

FRESH: MEATS & SEAFOOD

bay scallops

pancetta or bacon

sweet Italian sausages

OCCASIONAL ITEMS

eggs

heavy (double) cream

Parmesan cheese

make the most of your time

Once you have put together your weekly meal plan, you can start organizing your time. Do as much as you can in advance, so that your meals come together quickly at dinnertime.

■ **Stock up.** Keep your pantry well stocked. Whenever you use an item, try to replace it soon after so that you always have everything you need on hand for a quick pasta meal, such as those suggested on page 97.

■ **Shop less.** If you make a weekly meal plan, you will need to shop less frequently, usually no more than two or three times a week.

■ **Do it ahead.** Do as much as you can ahead of time. Many pasta sauces call for ingredients that can be rinsed and cut up several hours or even up to a day in advance. Some sauces can be partially cooked earlier in the day and then finished at dinnertime, while cooked tomato sauces and a handful of other sauces, such as meat ragù, can be fully made up to one or two days before serving. If you have extra time one night, make and serve a quick and easy recipe while you slowly simmer a ragù to serve on a night when you don't have spare time. Pasta soups can also be made a few days ahead, though the pasta itself should be cooked just before serving. See the tips that accompany many recipes for additional ideas on what you can do in advance.

■ **Double up.** When making a basic pasta sauce, make enough to use in different ways for more than one meal. For example, prepare a big batch of tomato-basil sauce and serve it over spaghetti one night. Later in the week, simmer meatballs in the sauce and serve it over pasta. Then, layer the rest of the sauce in a lasagna for a third supper.

■ **Cook smarter.** Read through the recipe before you begin, so you know all the steps. Then, clear your work space, assemble your equipment and prep your ingredients, arranging them on the countertop, and set the table. Whenever possible, enlist family members or guests to help with kitchen or dining-room tasks. By taking a few minutes to organize your space and ready your ingredients before you begin cooking, you will be able to prepare the recipe more quickly and efficiently.

the well-stocked kitchen

Smart cooking is all about being prepared. Keeping your pantry, refrigerator, and freezer well stocked and organized means you'll always save time when you are ready to cook. Get into the habit of regularly tracking what is in your kitchen and you'll find that you can shop less frequently and spend less time in the store.

What follows is a guide to the ingredients you'll need to have on hand for making quick and tasty pasta dishes, along with advice on how to organize and store them. Use these tips for a new, smarter approach to putting meals on the table. The time you spend organizing will pay off when it's time to make dinner: once your kitchen is stocked and organized, you'll be able to make any pasta dish in this book by buying just a few fresh ingredients.

the pantry

Your pantry may be a cupboard, a closet, or wherever you store your dried, canned, and jarred foods and such fresh ingredients as onions, garlic, and other produce items that do not require refrigeration. It should be cool, dry, dark when not in use, and away from the heat of the stove, which can hasten spoilage. For maximum freshness, rotate your pantry items and replace ingredients that are past their prime.

stock your pantry

- Take inventory of what is in your pantry using the Pantry Staples list.

- Remove everything from the pantry; clean the shelves and reline with paper, if needed; then resort the items by type.

- Discard items that have passed their expiration date or have a stale or otherwise questionable appearance.

- Make a list of items that you need to replace or stock.

- Shop for the items on your list.

- Restock the pantry, organizing items by type so everything is easy to find.

- Write the purchase date on perishable items and clearly label bulk items.

- Keep staples you use often toward the front of the pantry.

- Keep dried herbs and spices in separate containers and preferably in a separate spice or herb organizer, shelf, or drawer.

keep it organized

- Look over the recipes in your weekly meal plan and check your pantry to make sure you have all the ingredients you'll need.

- Rotate items as you use them, moving the oldest ones to the front of the pantry so they will be used first.

- Keep a list of the items you use up so that you can replace them.

USING DRIED HERBS

Fresh herbs, with their bright taste, are generally the best choice for flavoring pasta sauces, but some dried herbs can be used successfully, including rosemary, thyme, marjoram, oregano, and sage.

The flavor of dried herbs is concentrated, so always use a smaller amount of the dried herb than the fresh. To substitute dried for fresh, use the following:

1 teaspoon dried tarragon or sage = 1 tablespoon fresh

2 teaspoons dried oregano, marjoram, or thyme = 1 tablespoon fresh

1½ teaspoons dried rosemary = 1 tablespoon fresh

BUYING BROTH

The busy cook seldom has time to make homemade stock, but good-quality chicken, beef, and vegetable broth can be found in cans or aseptic boxes on market shelves, or in containers in the frozen-food section of many upscale markets, delis, and some butchers.

PANTRY STORAGE

Keep pantry items in small quantities so you restock regularly, ensuring freshness.

dried pasta The shelf life of most dried pasta is 1 year. Although it's safe to eat beyond that time, it will have lost flavor and can become brittle. Once you break the seal on a package, put what you don't cook into a resealable storage bag or an airtight glass or plastic container and return to the shelf.

olive oil Light and heat are enemies of olive oil, so always store your oil in a cool, dark place, in tightly corked or capped dark glass bottles. It will keep for about 1 year, but the sooner you use it, the better your oil will taste. To help keep your oil fresh, use a vacuum wine pump and a rubber stopper.

dried herbs & spices Store spices and dried herbs in airtight glass jars and label clearly, including the date of purchase, so you know when to replenish. Keep in a dark, cool, dry environment for no more than 6 months, after which they will have lost their potency.

fresh foods Check fresh pantry items—garlic, onions, shallots, some roots and tubers—occasionally for sprouting or spoilage and discard if necessary. Never put potatoes alongside onions; when placed next to each other, they produce gases that hasten spoilage.

canned foods Discard canned foods if the can shows any signs of expansion or buckling. Once you have opened a can, transfer the unused contents to an airtight container and refrigerate or freeze.

PANTRY STAPLES

DRIED HERBS & SPICES

bay leaves

black peppercorns

fennel seeds

marjoram

oregano

red pepper flakes

rosemary

sea salt and/or kosher salt

tarragon

thyme

white pepper

whole nutmegs

CANNED FOODS

chicken broth

chickpeas (garbanzo beans)

diced or crushed tomatoes

pink or pinto beans

tomato paste

white beans

whole plum (Roma) tomatoes

FRESH FOODS

garlic

lemons

shallots

white potatoes

yellow onions

SPIRITS

dry red wine

dry white wine

vodka

DRIED PASTAS

bucatini

capellini

cavatelli

conchiglie

ditali, ditalini

farfalle

fusilli

gemelli

lasagna

linguine

macaroni

orecchiette

orzo

penne

rigatoni

spaghetti

spaghettini

tagliatelle

tubetti

ziti

MISCELLANEOUS

anchovy fillets

black olives

brown lentils

capers

dried porcini mushrooms

extra-virgin olive oil

flour

green olives

olive oil

the refrigerator & freezer

Used for short-term cold storage, the refrigerator is ideal for storing fresh produce, meat, poultry, and seafood, as well as sauces prepared in advance and leftover pasta dishes. Done properly, freezing will preserve most of the flavor and nutrients of some foods and is especially recommended for storing certain types of pasta sauces that you want to keep for longer periods of time.

general tips

- Foods lose flavor under refrigeration, so proper storage and an even temperature of below 40°F (5°C) are important.

- Freeze foods at 0°F (-18°C) or below to retain color, texture, and flavor.

- Never crowd foods in the refrigerator, as air needs to circulate freely so items remain evenly cooled. Avoid packing foods too tightly in the freezer as well. The unbroken movement of air ensures that foods freeze more quickly, thus better preserving their flavor.

- To prevent foods from developing freezer burn, use only moistureproof wrappings, such as aluminum foil; airtight plastic and glass containers; or freezer-grade resealable plastic bags.

pasta sauce & soup storage

- Let pasta sauces and soups containing pasta cool to room temperature and then transfer to airtight containers. Refrigerate most sauces for up to 2 days and soups for up to 4 days.

- In general, cooked tomato-based sauces and other liquid-heavy sauces are good candidates for freezing. Let cool to room temperature and transfer to airtight containers in 2-cup (16–fl oz/500-ml) portions, for 1 lb (500 g) pasta. Leave 1 inch (2.5 cm) headroom to allow for expansion during freezing. Alternatively, pack in resealable plastic freezer bags, expelling as much air as possible before sealing. Be sure to write the type of sauce and the date on the container.

REFRIGERATOR STAPLES
Keep these everyday ingredients on hand not only for making pasta, but for all kinds of cooking. Then, when you're ready to make a recipe, you will need to buy only a few fresh ingredients, such as produce, meat, or poultry.

MEAT
pancetta or bacon

DAIRY
eggs
heavy (double) cream
milk
unsalted butter

CHEESE
fresh goat cheese
fresh mozzarella
Gorgonzola
Parmesan
pecorino

NUTS
hazelnuts (filberts)
pine nuts
walnuts

Once you have stocked and organized your pantry, you should apply the same basic principles to your refrigerator.

clean first Remove items a few at a time and wash the refrigerator thoroughly with warm, soapy water, then rinse well with clear water. Wash and rinse your freezer at the same time.

rotate items Check the expiration dates on refrigerated items and discard any that have exceeded their time. Also, toss out any items that look questionable.

stock up Use the list at the left as a starting point to decide what you need to buy or replace.

shop Shop for the items on your list.

date of purchase Label items that you plan to keep for more than a few weeks, writing the date directly on the package or on a piece of masking tape.

It's always a good idea to cook with wine you'd actually want to drink. Avoid any products labeled "cooking wine," which tend to be of poor quality.

Once a wine bottle is uncorked, the wine becomes exposed to air, causing it to oxidize. Left for too long, the wine will begin to taste like vinegar. Store opened wine in the refrigerator for up to 3 days. To slow down oxidation, use a vacuum wine pump to stopper the bottle.

fresh herb & vegetable storage

- Trim the stem ends of a bunch of parsley, stand the bunch in a glass of water, drape a plastic bag loosely over the leaves, and refrigerate. Wrap other fresh herbs in a damp paper towel, place in a plastic bag, and store in the crisper. Rinse and stem all herbs just before using.

- Store tomatoes and eggplants (aubergines) at room temperature.

- Cut about ½ inch (12 mm) off the end of each asparagus spear; stand the spears, tips up, in a glass of cold water; and refrigerate, changing the water daily. The asparagus will keep for up to 1 week.

- Rinse leafy greens such as chard, spin dry in a salad spinner, wrap in damp paper towels, and store in a resealable plastic bag in the crisper for up to 1 week. In general, store other vegetables in resealable bags in the crisper and rinse before using. Sturdy vegetables will keep for up to a week; more delicate ones will keep for only a few days.

cheese storage

- Wrap all cheeses well to prevent them from drying out. Hard cheeses, such as Parmesan, have a low moisture content, so they keep longer than fresh cheeses, such as mozzarella. Use fresh cheeses within a couple days. Store soft and semisoft cheeses for up to 2 weeks and hard cheeses for up to 1 month.

meat, poultry & seafood storage

- Most seafood should be used the same day you purchase it. Place clams or mussels in a bowl, cover with a damp towel, and use within a day.

- Use fresh meat and poultry within 2 days of purchase. If buying packaged meats, check the expiration date and use before that date.

- Place packaged meats on a plate in the coldest part of the refrigerator. If only part of a package is used, discard the original wrapping and rewrap in fresh wrapping.

index

weldonowen

415 Jackson Street, Suite 200, San Francisco, CA 94111
www.wopublishing.com

MEALS IN MINUTES SERIES
Conceived and produced by Weldon Owen Inc.
Copyright © 2006 by Weldon Owen Inc. and Williams-Sonoma, Inc.

The recipes in this book have been previously published as *Pasta* in the Food Made Fast series.

Color separations by Mission Productions in China
Printed by 1010 Printing in China

Set in Formata
This edition first printed in 2011
10 9 8 7 6 5 4 3 2 1

Library of Congress Cataloging-in-Publication data is available.

Weldon Owen is a division of
BONNIER

Photographers Tucker + Hossler
Food Stylist Kevin Crafts
Food Stylist's Assistant Luis Bustamante, Alexa Hyman
Prop Stylist Robin Turk

ACKNOWLEDGMENTS

Weldon Owen wishes to thank the following people for their generous support in producing this book: Davina Baum, Heather Belt, Ken DellaPenta, Judith Dunham, Marianne Mitten, Sharon Silva, Lesli Sommerdorf, and Kate Washington.

Julia della Croce would like to thank La Molisana Pasta, DiPalo Fine Foods, Rita Ghisu, Giustina della Croce, Annette Messina, Diane Miecnikowski, Anna Amendolara Nurse, Oswaldo Herrera, Sonia Berah, Gabriella della Croce, Celina della Croce, Judith Weber, and Kim Goodfriend.

Photographs by Bill Bettencourt: pages 8–9, 50–51, 54–55 (recipe), 60–61 (recipe), 74–75, 89 (lower right)

ISBN-13: 978-1-61628-222-6 (paperback)
ISBN-10: 1-61628-222-3

ISBN-13: 978-1-61628-254-7 (hardcover)
ISBN-10: 1-61628-254-1

A NOTE ON WEIGHTS AND MEASURES

All recipes include customary U.S. and metric measurements. Metric conversions are based on a standard developed for these books and have been rounded off. Actual weights may vary.